When The Gods Were Half Human

Kaelum Gaynes

Copyright © 2022 Kaelum Gaynes
All rights reserved.

Published in the United States by *Free Peanut Butter Press*

Trade Paperback ISBN: 978-1-958899-14-4
Hardcover ISBN: 978-1-958899-00-7
eBook ISBN: 978-1-958899-01-4

Cover design by Kaelum Gaynes

DEDICATION

*For every soul I've met on my journey
with their lamp lit to help me find my way*

CONTENTS

1
Morning musings over gravity

Hylozoism	2
A Short Course In Relativity	3
Metaxis	4
Suspended Animation	6
Eating Oatmeal	7
Fission	11
Blink	12
For Beauty	13
Wayfarers	14
Morning Meditation	16
Chromaticity	17

2
Never give a sword to a man who can't dance

Water, Thunder, Fire	20
Salat Al Zuhr	24
Chop Wood, Carry Water	25
When The Gods Were Half Human	29
Amaranthine	31
Revolution	32
Prometheus	34
Growing Up	35
God & Dust	42
Orthodoxus	44

3
In my heart, loud as thunder

Eurydice	46
Surgery	47
Heteronomy	50
Aphanitic	51
Lightning Over Iowa	52
Yab-Yum	54
Dakshina Kālikā	56
Black Magic	59
Kintsukuroi	60
Amends	61
Surrender	63
Athanasia	66

4
those that will not break it kills

Blood	68
In The Quiet Places	69
Enciente	70
Confines	71
Deism	72
Irrevocable	74
Sepulture	76
Old Wounds	78
Down	80
Death Dance	83

5
Whispers & Prayers

I'm Here	86
Syntropy	87
Mending	88
The Being Prayer	90
Apotheosis	91
Wait	93
Swan	96
Forevermore	98
Again	101

ACKNOWLEDGMENTS

Annika Knepper, I would not be the man I am without your unwavering commitment to embody truth, the courage to stand in your power and challenge me to keep reaching deeper in the finding of mine, and the inspiring artistry of your feminine essence finding its way in the world…you are poetry in motion.

Katie Kapugi, I would not be the writer I am without your mercurial genius to whet the blade of my creative expression. I'm profoundly grateful to you for challenging me as a writer and helping in the structuring, editing, and refining of this book.

Dayne Grove, our fellowship is a gift I will never take for granted. Your commitment to mastery without losing love has been a bright light in some very dark places for me, without which this book may have never seen the light of day.

Howard Cohen, your unwavering friendship and support has been one of the precious few constants in all the years we've known each other, it's hard to imagine those years—and the path to here—without you in them.

Anna Reedy, I couldn't get rid of you if I tried. That unshakeable love is a gift that has shaped me in undeniable ways over the last decade. Your companionship has been a catalyst for transformation in many seasons of growth, and as such your presence is a thread finely woven into the words of this book.

EPIGRAPH

The world breaks everyone and afterward many are strong at the broken places. But those that will not break it kills. It kills the very good and the very gentle and the very brave impartially. If you are none of these you can be sure it will kill you too but there will be no special hurry.

—Ernest Hemingway

Life is a lot of things…
I'm glad that beautiful is one of them.

— ONE —

Morning musings over gravity

Hylozoism

What language does the morning sun speak?

And were I given ears to hear,
would whatever utterance one might call
words mean as much in my sphere
as the concept of *morning*
must mean to the sun?

What thoughts do hydrogen
and helium think?

Are there measures of time
or distance in the vernacular of stars?

Could it not be that the musings of this
not-so-distant, massive being
are known to me as light
and heat?

Such that when that yellow dwarf thinks
its last thought…

I will also be thinking mine.

A Short Course In Relativity

Whatever it is that the spider steps on
I am too far up to see…

which leads me to wonder
what it is that might be

too far up to see the spider
but that must make the choice

to step on
or over

me.

Metaxis

There is a secret life I lead,
a secret kept from even me.

Filled with shapes and figures,
stories and scenes,
characters and creatures
my waking world has never seen.

Somewhere, while I am still
curling the soft fingers of my sleeping brain
through the little that remains
of some soon to be forgotten dream–

the slow morning sun seeping in through the seams
of my still-closed eyes–

the creatures of this dream are still alive.
Solid as stones. Secret as night.

So it seems worth asking
one question at the very least…

When I lay my human body down,
close my eyes and concede to the deep,
am I waking up in another world?

With memories of this one
that are not mine to keep?

Fumbling the clumsy fingers of my sedated brain
over the shapeless figures of a forgotten life
that's just out of reach?

Where the soft light of an unfamiliar star
is warming the walls of a world I could only imagine,

and I am waking into the dreams
my other half is having
while I am awake and he is asleep.

Suspended Animation

>Lying with the weight of me
>morning musings over gravity
>a soft rock in a shallow pond

>one sock off
>>one sock on

>before my sleep-soaked mind remembers
>that anything was ever wrong.

Eating Oatmeal

While I am writing this sentence,
finding my thoughts below the drone
of the apartment manager's vacuum
roaring outside my door,

boiling water to make oatmeal,

there are tens of thousands of orgasms
building to release.

After which, one or the other
will soon be asleep.

There are monks on mountaintops
seated and at peace, silent in their prayers,
promised not to speak.

While somewhere there are children
watching war outside their window
break out in the streets.

Right *now*
someone is drowning

while I am stirring my oatmeal.

And someone is pulling the lever that makes fire,
to push their hot air balloon yet higher.

Someone is building a fence.
…is putting their teeth in.
…is killing a chicken.

Someone is scuba diving in waters so deep
there is only the light of their lamp,

while someone else is planning a coup
in their war-torn world.

Someone, somewhere, is trying to milk a cow
that's already been milked,

while someone who's barely awake
is sewing the last patch on a hand-stitched quilt.

Someone has just been shot,
and someone else has watched.

Something someone else will never know
was happening, somewhere not so far away,
while they hovered above the bathroom sink
wetting the blade to shave.

Someone is learning a new dance
and feeling awkward
with their more experienced partner.

It seems inevitable to me, all things being equal,
all people being free…

that someone, somewhere, is seeing snow
for the very first time, and falling to their knees.

While someone else is squatting in the woods.
…is forgetting to take their pills.
…is praying to a god I have never heard of

and likely never will.

Someone is standing with the refrigerator door
half open, looking for something that isn't there,
but hungry for it still.

I am a single atom
in the universe of a billion suns,
eating my oatmeal

while someone is…

Fission

It would come on a morning like this.

The rain playing the leaves,
birdsong breaking in the day,
an early fall frost across
the sugar dusted lawn.

The neighbor's chimney is smoking.

One squirrel is scolding another for reasons
as secret as the stone-still lake.

The less kept secret is the whistle
of an overhead plane.
The inhale

and wait

for the thought to pass
that it would come on a day like today.

Blink

It's amazing how whole
worlds come to pass
with the opening
and closing
of eyes.

For Beauty

I wish that beauty
was a thing discussed by politicians
and heads of states,

perhaps it would feel less strange
to be here.

I wish that the balance of a thing—

> the cadence of color and line
> and the way it speaks of higher things
> that put the lower things in nice perspective—

was its start, not its finish.

I wish that all this was seen
not just from the fringes
but from the center,

where the hands would use the eyes to see,
and the work would be for beauty.

Wayfarers

Translucent tendrils of the yellow-flowered zucchini
are reaching. Shooting out in so many directions,
searching for contact, for something
that when touched…
touches back.

Some of them have arrived
at the cool, sturdy rung of the galvanized ladder
they are meant to climb,

spiraling like doodles on a page,
tiny green pythons worming
their soft whiskered bodies
tightly around the wire.

The rest of them,
softly bobbing on the wind,
strong and straight and calmly
keeping it all together,
floating in the empty air,
ever so slightly curled over
nothing but faith.

I whisper to them that I understand.
That all there is to do is keep reaching.
That they are not alone.

Morning Meditation

When the narrator forgets himself

all that's left are the shapes in the carpet,
the muffled chatter of nameless birds—

    all better at speaking than at listening—

and the warmth of tea.

Chromaticity

Longing is like the color red
on the poet's pallet.

Blue is the color of a wish
that may or may not come true.

Green for the things we've seen
that we wish we had not seen,

memories like balled up fists.
But all these colors must be mixed.

Nothing in life is so simple
as red or blue or green.
Primary colors are for children.

While black and white are for the broken mind
that survives and calls it life.

Whisper and the colors run.
Whisper and they bleed.
Whisper and call it all beautiful.

— TWO —

Never give a sword to a man who can't dance

Water, Thunder, Fire

In Feng Shui it is inauspicious to place your home
near a fast moving river, agitated by rapids

…it disturbs the chi.

And any Zen master of the modern age will tell you
that tall buildings reach like mountains,
busy highways rush like rivers.

I moved from the one-bedroom by the bank,
a stone's throw from the interstate,
wheels screaming night and day,
because of water.

~

The girl was practical,
all cloud, no rain…or so it seemed.
If you prefer words to feelings, (and I often do),
I recommend dating an Aquarius.
Just don't date one with a Cancer moon,
as there are no rules to say that one cannot drown
in the ocean beneath a clear blue sky.

I moved from our shared unit by the docks,
where we would eat seafood and watch the boats
catch and release the tension in their ropes,
because of water.

* * *

In the Bagua, the third trigram is Zhen…*thunder*.
It speaks of the East, wood, and all things green

…as well as family.

Because as thunder precedes the storm,
so are our ancestors the rumbling skies
that warned the world we were coming.

But the Bagua says nothing of the way a family can
rattle the window panes from their frames,
until there is nothing left between you and the world
but skin.

I left the home that holds my childhood
coin collection, still somewhere in the attic,
because of thunder.

~

Confucius tells us in all his wisdom
never to give a sword to a man who can't dance.

Wiser words have not been spoken.
So I also trust him when he says that silence
is a true friend who never betrays.

Though he must have died before
he could complete his esoteric writings
on how to get your upstairs neighbors to
take their shoes off in the house.

Not a single board in that floor could keep a secret.
Not the late night bowls of cereal
or all the Settlers of Catan marching quiet as
a herd of cattle across the kitchen table.

And certainly not the children,
rolling through the night like storm clouds
over the Oklahoma prairie, shaking
every beanstalk in the field to its roots.

I left the garage—where I laid down carpet
and slept with the door half open
to feel closer to the people I love—
because of thunder.

* * *

Thirty-three times I've moved
in thirty-three years.
The most recent being yesterday,
the day before my thirty-third birthday,

when my bedroom flooded,
and the California wildfires turned the sun to blood
and the air to ash…

I guess just to make sure that
I couldn't even sleep in my truck,
like I did last year for that one month
that turned into four.

It's hard not to think of poor Job,
how God rewarded his resilience.

And I wonder whether God is teaching me,
like all his people, that home will always be
just another place to leave…

or if He is just punishing me for studying Feng Shui
and reading Confucius.

Salat Al Zuhr

Arm over arm,
head hung towards Mecca

a rapt silence slicing
through the earthly realm

of parked cars and foot traffic
circumnavigating this man
in his concrete Mosque

covered knees kneeling
on the well-worn rug
laid down in the smallest sliver of shade

over space thirteen
of the paid lot across the street,
on the hard-packed black desert sand
of sweltering asphalt…

this secret meeting of one;
this thin pocket of sacred.

Chop Wood, Carry Water

Before enlightenment–

>*chop wood,*
>*carry water.*

After enlightenment–

>*chop wood,*
>*carry water.*

There is a sacred mundanity
that wraps itself around every greatness.

It is the mountain to the diamond.

Though we will be remembered
for our moments of grandeur—

our magnum opus…
our definitive novel…
the role we were born to play—

whatever power or potential there is
to achieve great acts
must be mined
from the raw materials
of a life well-lived.

It matters,
to the magnificence,
that you brush your teeth

…and *how*.

These moments of brilliance
are not plucked from the sky
into an otherwise infertile life.

They are the distillate of every act
of empathy, of self-care,
of risks taken— big and small.

They are the collected works
of the ones we love,
and the ways we've loved them;

of every meal made
and of every dish done.

Of the food we eat,
the love we make,
the places we visit
and the journeys we take.

Good art is painted
with the colors and strokes
of our daily lives,

with the moments when we are alone
and doing things of no real consequence
that will be remembered by no one.

These moments in the dirt are sacred
as our flowering reach for heaven.

It is this reaching
that is our *being*.

And the *being* that is the most dangerous,
courageous, ardent act of art there is.

If we are not that
then we are nothing
at all.

And so in the end,
though our greatness will save us
from mundanity,

the mundane will then save us
from our greatness.

When The Gods Were Half Human

Some wish their lives on different times,
golden ages on history's stage.

If only to have been there
when the cowboys slung their six guns
or when art, like Caravaggio, carried a sword

and cut the world in two.

I myself wish I could remember
when the gods were half human.
When life was meant to be spent, not saved

…and God was not so far away.

It was in the blood and the dust
and the edge of the blade,
where life was lost and life was made

…and God was not so far away.

It was in thunder and fire
and the ocean's rage,
where sins were washed in ancient waves

...and God was not so far away.

It was in sweat and semen
and savage embrace,
where light was lust and the wound could save

...and God was not so far away.

Amaranthine

History is a story of men wasting
stories, the slow erosion of
words steeped in the acid of rhetoric

Platitudes used to soften the symptoms
of the sharp and hard edges
of an uncertain existence

And yet
while skin and bones collapse in time,
broken and buried,
the *soul* breathes still

Into new bodies,
bodies for their age and hour,
for us to find and hold
and hope until they die

Beneath the amaranthine sky.

Revolution

Sometimes I am shattered all at once,
in the downswing of a single hammer
that falls to finish what a lesser man started.

And when I had been so reckless as to hope
that it might have instead been
a rising up, to swing the first nail
into something new.

But most often, hope bleeds out
one cell at a time,
through each invisible incision
of injustice, through each one
of a thousand tolerable acts…

until we are bloodless.

The whole machine is bloodless
but for faith, a dim light burning on the sill,
a single candle carried still
from room to room but ready

to burn the whole house down
in the kind of ruin that rises up
from the ashes of all we've ever known
to save us from ourselves.

Prometheus

Perhaps there are gods
who can hold fire in their hands
and not burn.

But in all the best stories I can call to mind,
the game is catch and release,
and the rise and the fall
are staggered in between.

It is the devil that lives in fire
…that would rather be transformed *by* it
than transform *with* it,

while the hero of any story
does not light a single match
without first a vision

for all that might rise
from rubble and ash.

Growing Up

As a young boy
I use to catch tadpoles
swim wiggling their sleek black bodies
at the still edges of a nearby stream,

drop them into the muddied water
of the plastic pet store terrarium
given out as a catch-all for living things
smaller than a human hand

and feed them fish food
until they sprouted tails
and *died*

...every time.

In summer, when the hot empty air of
evening filled itself with fireflies
flickering like tea lights,
suspended in ether slowly

burning and somehow still
as night, shooting embers
sleepy in flight

I would stand and imagine
my own little cosmos
slow-racing through time…

blink and a sky-full of stars is born,
blink again and all of it ends.

With an almost instinctive reverence
I would give my moment of silence to that
not so distant starry night

before *clapping* my hands to capture them,
sometimes two at a time.

If they were lucky they would live
in a mason jar with air holes poked in the lid,

lighting up my bedroom,
forgotten and fading like little flashlights
left on until the batteries ran dead.

If they were unlucky they would be smeared
like glow-stick goo on the sidewalk,
or on my skin to impress a friend.

I had not yet learned
that where there is light there is life.
That nothing is taken without cost…

even if we do not yet know what
that cost might be.

***

Once I knocked a nest full of birds
from its tree.

That was the day I learned empathy.

All those baby birds so helpless
and hungry, their mother up above
screaming down at me, weeping
over those naked cheeping bodies.

Something woke up inside me that day.
I had taken from Eden's tree
and with it the knowledge
of good and evil.

There is suffering outside of me.
There is suffering even in the smaller things.

***

Yesterday evening
I watched a documentary of U.S. history,
and imperialism in general.

Spain, France, Germany, China
…whoever could pay to play the game
of war and expansion, carving up the land
as if it were not a living thing that bleeds;

to say nothing of the people,
mowed down like weeds
to make flat the path for forks and Bibles
in one language or another.

Strangely, it was neither fury nor fear that I felt
as I watched this–

it was *confusion*.

How does one human being punch holes in another,
knowing this will cause all the life to leak out?

How does one human being steal the light
glowing in another's eyes, somehow not knowing
it could never make their own light any brighter?

It's just one less fire burning to light the path
that leads us all home.

And soon there will be no stars left in the sky
…only darkness.

***

I'm not sure it would be right to say
that we have lost our way, but rather, perhaps,
that like all things in their adolescence
we simply have not found it yet.

And that the purpose of our pain is to teach us respect.

That the value of a life cannot be measured in size, where the body that is bigger is worth more than the small,

where we would shake a nest from its tree just to feel our fists and watch it fall.

We think we are grown because we are further along than our fathers were, but it must be known
that we are not there yet…

when still the only way to know our strength
is to find what we can break,
and the only power we have is the power we take.

This innocence may be the end of us,
but if it is not that, then it is just the beginning.

* * *

They say that girls mature faster than boys.
The same way, I pray, that individuals
learn to *feel* faster than empires.

But someday,
and soon I hope,
we will all look *together*
at those naked cheeping bodies
and all the screaming mothers

and feel sorry.

God & Dust

Nature does not have the capacity
to transcend itself,

    and yet somehow we do.

You will never find a crow asking questions
for which the absence of answers
 empties a bottle.

Nature takes care of itself.
But who takes care of us?

A question only we have to ask.

And it's the answer that decides
if we will love our lives
or let go,

and build a hell
of our very own.

And yet *this* is where God is
mixed in our dust.

That we have the power
to breed the beast of hell;
and with that, heaven
is at our fingertips.

But only we can decide
which.

Nature takes care of itself.
But who takes care of us?

We do.

And when this is true,
that will be our heaven.

Orthodoxus

It is all true

And there is no truth
but *movement*.

The movement of many stories.
And even the best stories need to be told,
though they could never be more true
than silence, still
they stand inside our limp skin
and teach us how to move again.

But one must never forget,
they are not true or untrue,
they are only shaped
or shattered.

— THREE —

In my heart, loud as thunder

Eurydice

I breathe
but not the deep

I drink
but not the sea

I knew you once, my love,
you were the inside of me

Sometimes I go there still
with hopes to find your ghost

and set our hidden angels free

Surgery

I was thinking today about that first long weekend
we spent together, hearing you say

"I wonder if we'll have our first fight?"

like the child (more eager than anxious)
waiting for that first wiggling tooth to fall.

"I can't imagine what that would look like."

I said, thinking how ridiculous it would be
for me to think that we might never fight

…then thinking it anyway.

Although "fight" wasn't quite the right
word for whatever we imagined
this relational rite of passage might look like.

There are fists in fights. There are
broken things and forgetting.

So we agreed that a "kerfuffle"
is more likely what we might have.

…That seems so long ago.

Now I'm not sure either of those words are quite right.
"Surgery" I think is what I would call it.

And while still there are no fists
in surgery, there are knives.
Not the switchblade or the sword,
but the obsidian edge of the scalpel.

There is no unmeasured move of that blade,
not thrust or stab.

Just the soft, almost secret incision,
peeling back every atrophied layer of ego
that refuses to trust.

A "fight" seems precious, by comparison.

* * *

But what else is there?

It is for hemorrhage to kill us quickly
or metastasis to take its time.

That we would risk the knife at all—
bodies shaking to keep the hands steady—
is a love, before you, I had only dreamt of.

Though I would have mistaken this dream
for a nightmare, this I am certain of.

I would have woken up in a cold sweat,
gasping for breath, belly up and
begging for death…

But we may make it yet.

Heteronomy

    everyone is idiosyncratic
    when you get close enough,

    even the most pristinely whittled edges
    have been shaved with the shaking hand
    of another human body

Aphanitic

It's a touching game,
reaching for hands like lifting up seashells
searching for pearls

pulling, yes,
calcified ivory strings
marbling your petrified heart
with the rigid purity that remains
from spending so many days in the dark

canyons of the sea, that fiery deep
where souls are tested for their mettle

when that empty light finds
and fractures your once soft heart

then you are spit shallow,
pummeled by waves that speak two truths—
that you are so close to your feet on firm ground,
and that you are beaten while you are down

until there is nothing left but sand
and pearl.

Lightning Over Iowa

There is a place
where I *feel* the lightning
over Iowa.

Fire like ice
cracking the night
into the stillness of god's
and the devil's fight.

Where the two become one
with the match that strikes
to light the night-wild fire.

It shatters the atom then
reunites the divide.

In the hallow expanse
of that saturnine sky

…you and I collide.

And it is as much above
as it is below,

in the silent starless void
a single note—

you and I…explode.

A sun is born,

burning bright like the sky
when there is fire over Iowa.

But only when my eyes are closed.

Yab-Yum

In your bed your look at me,
you would rather play war with silence
than speak.

And while for part of me,
just what your face can say
is all I'll ever need,

there is another place
that plays the game for words,
getting answers to the questions I ask…
asking the wrong questions.

But eternity is not in your bed.

In eternity
we are tangled in legs,
eyes locked and tumbling
through galaxies
in yab-yum,

creating and destroying worlds,
infinitely being,

divine ecstasy
and wrath.

Dakshina Kālikā

You think that I would save you,
like the night from its darkness.
That given the chance I would
finish what Jesus started,
and level that darkness like the Amazon,
just to burn it for light.

You are wise to know
it is your gift to carry in this world
that spark of night, that primordial black sea
that runs in you dark as your waters are deep.

That runs from me…
because I come in peace.

You are the dark Goddess Kali,
four-armed destroyer with fire for a tongue
that would lick me to ashes
before my faith ever ran in your veins.

I think it's true,
that this world in its fight with the other side of life

would call your beauty broken,
would see you as some beast,
some disturber of the peace,

and so you lock yourself inside
the way all good demons do.

But you know what they don't…
that destruction is just the beginning
of birthing something new.

That life issues forth from the darkness
of that womb.

That the love of death *is* the love of life,
and that someone must speak
for the pain of the world

or that pain will speak for us.

What you *don't* know
is the life your night breathes in me.

I would dance in your shadows if you would let me,
to the music that plays in the fire in your eyes.

That medusa stare that would turn a lesser man to stone,
where my shadow-god is not alone.

But still,
you are afraid that I would take this from you
and make it *good*.

But all I am offering is to hold your hand.
To swim in your abyss and tell you you're beautiful.
To give whatever I can while you learn what it means
to be the night, to destroy

rather than be destroyed.

I am not the end of you,
I couldn't be if I wanted to.

There is no day without night,
and your darkness, my love,

…is your light.

Black Magic

Sorceress, sibyl, siren and muse,

buckle me under your magmatic pull,
where the wild fire is both
eros and calcine.

I am not fury nor fervor,
I am the dissolution of the two,

the skin-stripped bones
that bow to you.

Kintsukuroi

I am shattered with the hammer
of life and death that you are

desperate for them both

filled with whatever you give
broken by all of it

and *whole*

in ways only a broken man
could understand

Amends

Remember the time you told me you might not want this,
just to know that you could,

and I cried for a week even after you realized
you were being foolish?

I remember when I couldn't cry at all,
before I met you…

when it would just sit down there
like all the chewing gum I'd ever swallowed,
stuck to my ribs, not letting the air in,
not letting life begin again.

And then, sitting in the car outside the co-op,
my body finally decided that someone really cared,
that there was a place in the world for all those tears.

You with cupped hands holding me in your lap,
all the life rushing back.

Now I can't stop.
Now I cry at movies about cartoon rabbits.

Now I remember that part of being alive is getting hurt,
and that's how all this started in the first place,
and it doesn't just stop now because I paid my dues.

When you said you weren't sure, it nearly broke me,
in the way that living things break.

But living things also bend,
and they also mend,

so I've got that going for me again.

Surrender

Today, I just miss you.

It's not the idea of you I miss,
or some fantasy of a risk-free reality
…some certain tomorrow, built on you
pretending to know what the future holds
and promising to hold me there.

Today, I just miss whatever it is
that makes you you.

Whatever's left when the cameras are off
and all the stories have been told,
and there's nothing left of the idea
that to have is to hold.

Even when we do not speak
there is love like the blood
you forget until you bleed.

But I've been holding on so tight for so long
I couldn't possibly have known,

this love is not just blood…
it's bone.

And that some secret part of me would rather break
than learn to be okay alone.

But I am choosing love, now,
and letting it break me
instead of you.

What is left is just to learn
what I somehow always knew,
that you cannot hold what
you cannot really lose.

~

Today, I just miss you.

But it's not because you're not already here,
it's because you are…

in some parallel universe,
in some uncertain now,
wrapped up in my arms somehow.

Today, my love, I just miss you.

But it's not because you're not already here,
it's because you are…

in my heart loud as thunder,
quiet as the rain,
soft as the wave-worn sands
where water has whittled the rock to silt
from pain

…and somehow only love remains.

Athanasia

I am nothing
more than the story,

teasing the strands of forgotten worlds,
watching the night sky for clues

from these long ago lives
that somehow live in me still.

There is no doubt of mine
that you and I have told many stories

and have many more to tell…

and that whatever comes of these lives—
past, present, future

and in all the alternate realities
and parallel universes on repeat—

you will echo in my blood and bones
through eternity.

— FOUR —

*Those that will not break,
it kills*

Blood

I want to know every pocket and canyon
where blood runs still,

where eccentric men have paced
and traced the steps of no one before them

bleeding from their bare feet dragging
on the jagged edges of an uninspired world.

My body runs bloodless for days,
often weeks, sometimes *months*

when there are no words,
when there is no skin,

no hidden world to take me in…
just this weather-worn body wasting

in the absence of ardor.

In The Quiet Places

there are lazy days
inside broken bodies
there are fires

fine particles suspended
in the emptiness of the unimagined

there is a suddenness
to its incantation

swell, billow, pulse

it must be noted
this emptiness is as much darkness

as it is light.

Enceinte

What is it you hold in hidden places…
secrets balled up like bulbs
buried under scorched earth.

When I look at you I see what you see—
dried soil stripped of life, swirling dust
writhing over baked red clay becoming
mudstone.

When I look at you I see
what you are too afraid to see—
untouched and untouchable
is a beautiful chaos,

a child this world couldn't take,
sinking deeper towards the surface,
given up

and waiting for the rain.

Confines

Which of us is the gorilla
that threw the old man at the wall,
that beat him with chains until he was
spineless.

Which of us lives behind the string
pulled taut on the swinging sign
warning: *do not touch*

and the glass that can't be tapped
or it will remind the animal
it was alive once

and nothing has changed.

Which of us would love
what we have nearly killed,
and which of us is nearly dead.

Deism

    I have lived two lives,
    one where there was nothing but
    sap-stained fingers and raspberries
    lifted from the neighbor's garden.

    Then another,
    when there was nothing
    but burnt trees and black magic
    and the shell-shocked child that stands there still.

    Time can be measured in either direction
    from the center.

    Then,

        there was the smell of burning leaves
        crackling in the yard, that we had
        been sure to pile high and swim in
        before sending up to God.

Then,

> there were cupped hands holding
> frog seeds pulled from the pussy willows,
> jet black and jumping with life.

Then,

> there were cracks of fire that lit the sky,
> warning the voice of a God
> I still believed in.

But fire does not live in the sky
of an indiscriminate God

who scorched the night,
who spit the seeds,
who lit the leaves

that burned the house down.

Irrevocable

    home is the packed snow
    where the white field slopes
    to shape the bank that made the
    quiet cave from winter's stone

    home is the yellow fence between
    the pool my brother did not drown in
    and the smooth black path to everywhere

    lit with the lightning of a thousand
    aimless faeries, floating soft as ash
    in the summer's still night

    home is the sap-stained hands rattling
    each rung of the birch-branch ladder
    to the top of the world

    it is the hill I used to mount my brother's bike
    before my legs could reach

the crackle of pine cones
beneath calloused feet

purple lilac swimming the wind
between me and the walnut tee

home is then, but has been nowhere since,
and it is either madness or love

that I am still looking

Sepulture

There is a brief moment
when winter has whispered to fall
and fall has whispered to summer
and summer buckles its bitter,
crisp, sigh of relief

When the air is a heavy blanket
tucked to the chin

And darkness rides in like a white knight
to quell the endless days of summer

When the turning of the leaves is,
somehow, a call to remember

But it is such a short time
before that blanket tucks you in too tight,
and the long days of summer lose
the will to light the day at all

There is a brief moment
when all there is to whisper has been said
and all there is to die is dead

And the trees, now naked as I am,
begin bearing down for yet another burial.

Old Wounds

There is an unspoken friendship
with the brittle stocks and fallen
seed heads holding their breath

beneath the bright white
and burnished death.

It is all inhale
and hold

in winter…

when the world waits
with me.

Come spring, the fiddleheads will
fester and stem from the furrow,
and I will be still
packed in the wind slab snow
of one winter, very long ago.

But today is a frozen day,
and that makes me
just another bear in its cave,

stirring in the wounded slumber
of winter's weathered wait.

Down

I am obsessed with what is below,
in the dark waters unknown.

My fingers were chopped from the wood
as a boy, as I clung to the boat.

Salvation, for me, has never been up.

It has always been
down.

It has had as much to do with angels
as with demons.

…And then there's Jesus.

Was there any *up* in his salvation?

For him it was always
down.

Down
from holy communion with his Heavenly Father.

Down
from the hope in men.

Down
from the mount at Golgotha,
shrouded and buried by Joseph of Arimathea.

From here there is no way up
but *down,*

deeper into life
until life becomes death
and death becomes something altogether

spectacular.

Heaven is a place.
        Salvation…a process.

Heaven is at the end of this
long road *down*,

and you will not know yourself when
you arrive there,

death will take that from you
…and that will be your heaven.

Death Dance

It's a tearing of limbs in the wilderness,
this death dance down.

This tribe of one
beating its drums and swinging
fire to burn the night.

I *am* the night.

I am the ghost tree that whispers
balmy in the black, standing
unmoved and rattling.

I am the demons swirling
formless and hysterical,
undead and unseen.

I am the howl and snarl
of the circling beast,
head under hackles and hungry.

I am everything but faith,
that when limb has been torn from limb
and scattered to the four winds,

something will remain.

— FIVE —

Whispers & Prayers

I'm Here

    if only for a moment
    if only as a thought
    if only as a specter reflecting

    some far beyond.

Syntropy

Some things cannot be spent
only whittled to dust,
smeared like ashes
on burnt skin stretched
over tired foreheads,

but nonetheless
it is a sign of hope.

Mending

Skin
is where I end
and the world begins,

but I am more than this.

I know that I am one shard
of a shattered God,
and that as I am

I am not.

I know that for every cell that divides
there is nothing but
to re-unite.

All of us lost in the spaces
of this divine divide.

There is something to be said
for learning to be separate,
in the same way that I am grateful
for who has become of the breaking,

the ways and places where life has been
less giving than taking.

So I will not call God foolish
for the devil They've made,
but neither will I sing as the Psalmist
that the Lord is my shade.

It is mending but it is broken,
and the break is the fissures of space
that run between skin,
and the saints that call the becoming
of whole again sin.

Everything I do that gets me closer to you,

and you are the rest of me
or I am the rest of you,

is all there is to do.

The Being Prayer

Help me remember
that I have a will,
the weight of which
the world can bear.

Help me remember
the animal inside.

Help me remember
that there is call
and response,

and that I am both.

Help me remember
that what I want will make me,
if I will let the reaching wake me.

Apotheosis

I don't owe this world a thing,
but I have found this hard to believe.

What life do I live
if not the one I *should*...

And how not to drown
in the endless ocean of all I *could*.

But I will learn to swim.
I will learn to walk in ways
I somehow never did.

I will make my own footprints in the sand
and they will not lead to Calvary,
they will lead to where they land.

I will lead,
but not because you follow.

I will give,
but not because you need it.

I will master the task of being alive,
but not because you see it.

I will *be*.

This world was broken when I got here
and it will be broken when I leave,
but I will leave the light on when I go.

That much I can do.
That much…I would be happy to.

Though it will not be what I gave,
it will be who I *became*.

Hate me
or love me…

my gift is my becoming.

Wait

Wait.

It will come.

But when

does the fallen pine find
the will to rise again?

How deep must it go
through the moss and soil?

How long must it rest (and rightly so)
before death stops being death?

Before that Great Wheel turns
and the spark of life ignites
again…

Wait.

                    Exhale.
Empty
and be true to it.

Revel in that darkness.
Dare it to keep you.

Know the end as the beginning
and death is not death,

only time.

Just look at the buckled pine,
fallen bridge to the stars.

It will (in it's own time)
rise

again, it will send up from its side
a child…

standing on that bridge,
reaching for those stars.

Wait.
> It seems still now.

It is.

But nothing is still forever,
and it is all worth the

wait.

Swan

How do I touch
to *feel* again?

How do I know the bones
that prop me up?

The skin
that holds me in?

The breath
that teaches me to count
...of life's *in* and *out*,

and that I am not so different
from the wind?

How do I sit,
just sit,

and let the noise become the stranger?

Teach me how to turn,
how to fall,
how to dance
or just to *swan*.

Teach me how to ebb
and flow,
how to mourn
even as I am laughing.

Teach me how to *be*,
even if unseen,
eternal and giving.

Forevermore

I am your blue,
your red,
your wild violet.

I am your dangerous,
your beautiful,
your ecstatic dance.

I am your stillness,
your patience,
your wisdom laughing.

I am your luminous,
your darkness,
your lunar pull.

I am your warmth,
your kiss,
your fiery abyss.

I am your cadence,
your fall,
your lapping at the shores.

I am your restlessness,
your quake,
your putrid reformation.

I am your romance,
your spring,
your every little thing.

I am your remembrance,
your folly,
your unrequited love.

I am your sprouting,
your doubting,
your gaseous expanse.

I am your gunshot,
your grief,
your ripping at the seams.

I am your moon-song,
your loss,
your twirling galaxies.

I am your whitecaps,
your worn,
your worlds beneath the sea.

I am your seething,
your teething,
your bubbling cauldron.

I am your limping,
your lurching,
your silent searching.

I am your depth,
your breadth,
your electric blue.

I am everything that ever was
and nothing
but *you*.

Your reverie,
your laughter,
your livid and your lore…

forevermore.

Again

Begin
the way the seed splits
and potential gives way to form.

Feel
the edges of existence,
the density that defies your infinite,

that contains you.

You could kick against it or touch
with it, at first, the black earth;
then green lit blades;
empty air bleeding
into clouds.

It tells you 'no'
as much as it gives you hands
to make that timeless will manifest.

Become
what you've never been...

what only time and touch and the faith
that what breaks will mend
can make you.

And when that is done...

End.
But don't just end
 ...end well.

End the same way you began,
different only in what you've become.

Dream your last dream in the silk sky.
Let the empty air fill your hollow body
one last time.

Let those green lit blades do their work
to break you
 down and back
  to that black and heavy earth

that not so long ago
spit you out.

Let it feed itself again.
Because a beginning is only as good as its
end.

Then,
if in life you found it
in you to believe

that all that breaks will mend,
        take a deeper breath yet
                and know that all endings begin

again.

ABOUT THE AUTHOR

Kaelum Gaynes

is a peripatetic bohemian warrior poet most often found somewhere between Southern California and Seattle. He is a writer of poetry, children's books, creative non-fiction and music. His work, fueled mostly by existential crisis and matcha lattes, commonly seeks to facilitate discourse (both internally and culturally) to stoke the glowing embers of humankind's reach for higher expressions of collective existence. Raised in the Midwest within a fundamentalist evangelical ideology, Kaelum had his first existential crisis at the age of 18 and subsequently made a life-long habit of it. His formal studies of Historical Theology and Western Philosophy, as well as Eastern Philosophy and Taoist Medicine, have informed an ever-expanding (and profoundly humbling) worldview, a tireless commitment to question everything, and a fundamental shift from *thinking* to *feeling*. In all his exploration he has come to believe two things with absolute certainty, that the truth of the Universe can be found wearing many different faces in the values, myths and religions of all races, cultures and creeds throughout history…and that *you will know the truth, and the truth will set you free*. If you are not free yet, your truth is not yet complete.

STAY CONNECTED

Changing the world starts with *thinking* different and ends with *being* different…with whole worlds of ingenuity in between. Art- like all things- is relational. It is the breathing between the artist, the art, and the perceiver. It is dynamic and alive; as much what you make it as what I do. So I give this book to you not as a product to be consumed, but as a gift to be received in your own way. It is what I have to offer, and as such, it is an invitation to *participate*…as all life is.

Releasing this book into the world is not an impersonal task for me, nor is it one-sided. Because all art is a dialogue, this book is simply a conversation starter. Some of the ways you will "respond" will be lived, they will *become* you in secret ways no one else will ever know. I have also created a few— more literal ways— to respond…to join the conversation and to engage in building community. These ways are listed in the pages ahead. I hope to hear from you!

Thank you for being a part of this.
It would be nothing without you.

1. JOIN MY MAILING LIST

Subscribe and be the first to know about new releases and upcoming events!

KaelumGaynes.com/connect

2. JOIN THE COMMUNITY!

I wanted a way to build sincere relationships with my audience, to facilitate community around shared values and personal growth…but I didn't want to use Facebook (or any other mainstream social media platform that's monetizing our attention, rife with dissent and distraction). I wanted to create an online space safe enough to foster authenticity and vulnerability— real human connection. So I created my own social media network, in an online community called The KG Collective, to do just that. This is a space where we can interact, share what these poems mean to you, ask me questions, write poetry together and more! There's a lot of potential in how this community can grow and evolve. I would love for you to be a part of it!

Type the below invite link into your browser to join the group!

kg-collective.us

3. FOLLOW ME ON IG

As mentioned above, mainstream social media platforms are not my jam, but Instagram provides an easy and accessible way for me to share poetry, animation projects and new releases.

@DirtySpirituality

4. EMAIL ME

While the KG Collective community is the best way to engage, email has its place as well. Depending on how much is going on in my life I may not be as quick to process emails but if you want to drop me a line that way, here's how.

Touch@KaelumGaynes.com

WANT TO ORGANIZE AN EVENT?

I am an independently published author and as such it is not the corporate resources of a large publishing house that are scheduling book tours to promote my work, it's you sharing my book with your friends. So if you're inspired by my writing and you have a community, work for a local book store, or have any other ideas about hosting an event to share my work and promote my writing, feel free to reach out via the email address below. Thank you!

Events@KaelumGaynes.com

CALL AND RESPONSE
(Send me a poem!)

Poetry- much like sneezing- can be hard to see someone else do without getting the itch to let one of your own rip. I've noticed over the years that when my writing has been dormant for a stretch, nothing gets the juices flowing again like the inspiration of other poets. At first I thought this was unique to me, but over the years I've noticed that when I share my poetry with others, they will often feel inspired to write one or two of their own. Nothing could be more rewarding to me than my art moving someone else to make theirs. It's a call and response!

One day, while reading a friend's poem- seeing how lit up she was to share it, and standing in amazement at how *good* it was- I thought to myself what a fun project it would be to compile a book of poems that have been written in response to mine. This is not a project for poets looking for a publisher, this is for the person who will sit down one lazy Sunday and write one of the few poems they'll ever write, then tuck that scribble-ridden notebook into a dark-lit closet never to think of it again. Because the difference between writing a poem and being a poet is hours and hours and years and years of work building a platform and an audience to share those poems. I've done that work, and what better way to appreciate my fans than to publish *their* poetry!

I don't know how long it will take to compile enough for a full book, and I can't guarantee I will publish every poem I'm sent. (I don't publish every poem *I* write either.) My vision is to create a cohesive body of work, a beautiful and diverse tapestry of voices.

Please note, the purpose of this exercise is to engage in a dialogue, a call in response. I'm sure there's a lot of amazing poetry out there, but for now the criteria for this project is collecting poetry that's been written in *response* to what I've written. It doesn't have to be in response to any particular subject matter I've written about, it can be about anything under the sun that you feel moved to write about. The "response" is simply that you wrote it with the inspiration stirred in you from something in this book.

Your poem can be shared within the KG Collective in the Space labeled **#Call-And-Response**.

Use a hashtag to indicate the work of mine that your writing is in response to, with titles consisting of multiple words strung together (ie: #deathdance). This will allow us to utilize the Highlighted Hashtags tab to organize these writings by the 'call' to which they are a 'response'. It will be fun to compare the diversity of ways that a single work of art can move uniquely through us.

www.ingramcontent.com/pod-product-compliance
Lightning Source LLC
Chambersburg PA
CBHW031139090426
42738CB00008B/1149